Stop Thinking Like an Employee

Stop Thinking Like an Employee

From Surviving to Thriving

A new approach to help you thrive at work and breathe life into an unfulfilled career

Marianne Renner

Copyright © 2021 Marianne Renner

All rights reserved. No part of this publication may be reproduced, stored in a retrieval system, or transmitted in any form or by any means – electronic, mechanical, photocopy, recording, scanning, or other-except for brief quotations in critical reviews or articles, without the prior written permission of the publisher.

ISBN: 9798775611088

This book is available for quantity discounts for bulk purchases.

For additional information about Marianne Renner Coaching Solutions, visit: MarianneRenner.com

or email:

Marianne@MarianneRenner.com

Contents

Preface 1

INTRODUCTION 5

Chapter 1
Consultant vs. Employee Mindset – As you Give . 9

Chapter 2
Give Your Attention 21

Chapter 3
Give Solutions 31

Chapter 4
Give the L-Factor 39

Chapter 5
Give Gratitude 51

Chapter 6
Give Your Gifts. 61

Chapter 7
Putting it all together 75

Conclusion 79

Additional Resources 83

About the Author 85

Preface

Let me guess. Right now, you have a job that feels draining. You have little energy or enthusiasm around the work you do. Getting up in the morning takes every everything you've got because you know the day ahead will drag on just like the day before.

OK, maybe it's not that bad. Perhaps getting up for work is more like having a pebble in your shoe. It's an annoyance – a constant low-level hum of discomfort. But it's not painful enough to change.

Either way, you dream about the next great thing. Maybe it's a business of your own. Or perhaps you're searching for that dream job, a leadership role, or something that allows you to use your gifts, talents and skills in an exciting way.

How did I know?

This is where many of my coaching clients are when they come to me. It's where I once was, too.

"Help me get out of my current situation," my clients plead, without knowing exactly where they want to go.

There are others who know where they want to be, but they seem to come up short. They come in second in the job interview. They're overlooked for the promotion. They always seem to be missing that one necessary skill set.

I've had the privilege of helping countless professionals break free from seemingly impossible situations. In some cases, they thought they could never earn their current salaries doing work that brings them joy.

Others worried that a lack of formal education or advanced degree would prevent them from getting the promotion.

For some, it was a story of limiting beliefs such as "I'm too young," or "I'm too old."

I've had many clients overcome the obstacles. They achieved what seemed to be impossible. They found work they love while earning unprecedented income.

Not all my clients have found their way to that happy ending. But for those who did, there were common themes.

From all the coaching conversations I've had over the years, I've seen clear patterns and trends emerge. When clients followed a particular set of behaviors, success was imminent. It happened too many times to be a coincidence.

What are those behaviors?

They learned to think and act like business owners, rather than employees.

This is what I call the consultant vs. employee mindset. An employee mindset focuses on what you get. A consultant focuses on what you give. Those who succeeded in finding more joy and fulfillment in their work learned to develop the consultant mindset.

I'm writing this book because I know what it's like to feel like you're meant for so much more, yet not being able to achieve it.

I also know the feeling of freedom and joy that comes from finding your sweet spot. It's that space where the work you're doing feels as natural and rewarding as a long, deep breath of fresh mountain air.

I want you to know there is a path for you. I found it, and I want to help you find it too. Believe me when I say, there is a way out of the chaos, even when you're unclear about where you want to go.

When you learn the secret to adopting the consultant mindset, doors open up that you never would have predicted. The unexplainable happens. A job opportunity seems to fall out of the sky. You get assigned to a new team or project that breathes life into what once felt stale. An old colleague calls you up with an exciting idea.

I've seen all of it happen as a result of adopting the consultant mindset.

You are made for a purpose. You have unique skills, gifts and abilities that are yours alone. There is no one else who can replicate what you have to offer. No one else can add value to an organization, a community or the world exactly the way you can.

Your value is as unique as your fingerprint.

If you don't shine in only the way you can, you'll deprive the world of your unique gifts.

In the pages ahead, you're going to find a combination of inspiring stories along with practical steps to guide you out of the current chaos and into a future filled with enthusiasm, energy and excitement. You'll lean into your unique gifts and gain a new sense of fulfillment.

You'll also find a number of additional resources in the back of the book to help you develop a more empowering mindset such as my Limiting Beliefs Worksheet, 4 Ways You May Be Sabotaging Your Success, and 2 free chapters to my Chaos to Clarity Success Journal.

MarianneRenner.com/belief

MarianneRenner.com/sabotage

STOP THINKING LIKE AN EMPLOYEE

MarianneRenner.com/journal

One thing I don't cover in this book is the value of hard work and competence. Those two characteristics are assumed here. It's a given that you're competent, as are so many of your counterparts. What we're diving into here are characteristics that will help you stand up, stand out and rise above the rest.

This is a book about mindset. The work before you is an inside job – one that occurs deep beneath the surface.

The steps ahead are simple, but they're not always easy.

This book is intentionally short and simple. It by no means covers everything you need to know to land your dream job. But if you follow even these simple steps, you'll experience a change.

Before you turn the page, let me ask one question: are you ready? Are you ready to do the work? Are you willing to try new things that may feel counterintuitive to everything you've done so far?

The hardest work you'll have to do is change the way you think.

After all, your best thinking got you to where you are today. Are you ready to think a little differently? Are you ready for a breakthrough?

If the answer is yes, you're half-way there.

Let's go!

INTRODUCTION

Have you ever wondered why other people seem to land the great job, the promotion or big success in business? What would it take to get yourself included in that "other people" category?

One of the best ways to stand out is to think like a business owner and develop what I call "the consultant mindset."

Most people go to work with an employee mindset, which means they spend much of their time thinking about what they want to get from an organization. If you tried this approach in a romantic relationship, that relationship would fizzle quickly.

We all know the importance in any great relationship of caring about the other person. In return, you are more appreciated and acknowledged. You reap the rewards.

The same is true in the workplace. When you show up looking for ways to serve and add value, you reap the rewards.

This is how the best business owners think. They focus on how they can add value to their customers.

Believe it or not, you are in business for yourself. You are in the business of creating work that is meaningful, fulfilling and financially rewarding. You are in the business of adding value for your biggest client, who in this case just happens to be your organization.

The chapters ahead will provide basic steps to help you think like a business owner and develop the consultant mindset. You will learn how to become more valuable in the workplace by using your unique skills, gifts, talents and abilities.

And if you're not sure about your unique skills and gifts, you'll find help with that here, too.

Throughout the book, you'll read real-life stories of clients who learned to apply the consultant mindset. Their names have been changed to protect confidentiality of my clients. In some cases, identifiable details have been changed. But their stories and outcomes are 100% true.

You'll find action steps at the end of each chapter to help you move forward in your journey.

These action steps are vital to finding more meaning and fulfillment through your work.

I encourage you to take your time with the action steps. Reflect on the questions. Spend time on your answers. The consultant mindset will require a shift in your thinking. It might feel counterintuitive and a little uncomfortable. You'll work to change some habitual thought-patterns and limiting beliefs.

Think of this book as part instructional, part inspirational, and part workbook.

You'll read instruction on how to develop and apply the consultant mindset. You'll read inspirational real-life stories of those who figured it out.

And finally, the end of each chapter provides space for you to document your action steps and journal additional notes. You'll also find additional blank pages at the back of the book for notes.

Write your thoughts. Journal your successes. Take note of what you tried to do differently and the outcome you experienced.

You'll find it valuable to track your experiences and your progress.

And oh, what fun it will be to go back and see how far you've come!

Chapter 1

Consultant vs. Employee Mindset – As you Give

I spent a long career as a high-performing employee. I worked hard. I was better than average at my job. I earned glowing performance reviews and high accolades from my leaders.

As far back as my college days, I thrived on the idea of overachieving. As a journalism major in college, I earned a prestigious role of editor on the campus daily newspaper. I had a byline above the fold of the Chicago Tribune by the time I was 21, which was a pretty big deal in those days.

Upon graduation, I landed a reporting job for a daily newspaper in a mid-sized market – another coup for a new college grad.

Shortly after that, I earned the title of Marketing Director for a business consulting firm and later transitioned into healthcare marketing, with a few stops in between.

My career was more of a zig-zag corn maze than a perfect career ladder, but I consistently performed above average in every role.

Nevertheless, I was unfulfilled at every stop along the way. I was good at what I did but something was missing. It was like wearing a pair of shoes that didn't quite fit. I got around ok. But I was never comfortable.

STOP THINKING LIKE AN EMPLOYEE

What's more, I felt overlooked when it came time to advancing in an organization. My salary creeped along with an annual cost of living adjustment or an occasional 2% bonus for a job well-done.

I asked for a promotion. I asked for more vacation time. I asked for salary increases.

I asked.

I asked.

I asked.

It never worked.

The more I focused on what I wanted to get, the more my efforts eluded me like a distant mirage.

It wasn't until I owned a business that I started to understand the error of my ways.

I had an employee mindset.

What's wrong with that? Afterall, I was an employee. What other mindset *should* I have?

As a business owner I learned that my "job" was to help my clients solve their problems. The more I could do that, the more value I was to my clients.

The more value I offered, the more my business grew. A-ha!

Biggest Client

If my business grew as a result of adding value to my clients, would the same thing happen in a traditional employed position?

The answer was, yes!

What if you approached your job as though you were a business owner, with your organization being your biggest client? What if you continually looked for ways to add more value to your customer, i.e., your boss, team and other leaders in the organization?

Could you identify a problem in the organization and offer a solution using your unique talents, gifts and abilities?

That's the role of any consultant. A consultant comes in to an organization, identifies a problem, then offers a solution to that problem. The more a consultant gives to its client, the more valuable he or she becomes.

An employee mindset focuses on what you *get*.

A consultant mindset focuses on what you *give*.

The employee says, I want to *get* more vacation time, more money or a lighter workload that seems fair.

A consultant asks, "how can I *give* more? How can I add value to the organization or customer? How can I better serve and use my unique talents and skills to help solve the problem at hand?"

The employee mindset asks "how can you help me?"

The consultant mindset asks "how can I help you?"

It really is that simple.

What if you stop worrying about what you want to get from an employer? If you focus on giving, the receiving is imminent.

It's a paradox, for sure. In fact, it feels counterintuitive.

If you want to receive more from your employer or customers, start with giving. A wise person once wrote, as you give you receive.

In the coming chapters, we'll look at keys to developing the consultant mindset that all have to do with giving.

Steven's Story

Steven came to me one day with an all-too-common story.

STOP THINKING LIKE AN EMPLOYEE

To put it in his words, "work sucked."

Steven worked for a small construction company that provided custom wood-working for high-profile commercial clients that included hospitals, schools and libraries.

"I begrudgingly went to work every day, feeling like I could never do enough and never get it right. The bosses were demanding, and the environment was unfair," Steven recalled. "It felt like my hands were tied, and I had no control. At least, that's how it seemed in my mind."

Steven was an experienced wood-working craftsman, having worked in the industry for 20 years. He felt unappreciated at work. In his opinion, his expertise went unnoticed and his ideas fell on deaf ears.

As a result, he and his co-workers would spend their time swapping stories about the injustices of the daily grind at the company.

"All the talk was about what was wrong with our employer," he said. "As strange as it sounds, it felt comfortable. It was like we were building walls around us that kept us in our comfort zone of complaining."

I asked Steven to start rebuilding new walls and to change the narrative. I asked him to describe an ideal day. What would it look like if he could design his dream job?

The vision

Steven began to dream. "I'm a master craftsman. Someday I'd like to create a team of master craftsmen, and I would be their leader. I don't know where. I don't know how. But they would be students of the craft. And I would become more and more proud of the work I do."

His eyes began to sparkle as he built this new vision in his mind.

Steven's idea was to start his own business. This would give him the control he was looking for to use his expertise in a way that created a deeper sense of significance. It would give him the freedom to surround himself with others who had the same high-level skills and desire to create high-quality products.

I asked Steven how he would show up as a business owner. How would he treat his team? How would he serve his biggest clients?

He told me about his heart to serve and deliver the highest value for his clients. He talked about how he would motivate, teach and inspire his team.

He described how he would share his gifts and talents as an experienced wood-working craftsman.

Consultant vs. Employee mindset

That's when I asked the big question. "What if you could show up like that right now and bring that mindset to your current job? What if you thought of yourself as a business owner, and your employer as your biggest client?"

He looked at me with inquisitive eyes. Then he replied, "That's exactly what I'll do.

He explains, "I went to work with an extra spring in my step. I walked a little higher. With that new mindset, I felt like I actually could make a difference."

With a consultant mindset, the first thing Steven did is get on board with the vision of his leadership. "I told them, 'I want you to know I'm on board with you. I'm here to help you with your dream of getting this shop where you want it to go.' There was no more, 'me vs. them.' I was 100% with them," Steven said.

STOP THINKING LIKE AN EMPLOYEE

He broke outside the walls of his comfort zone. He no longer commiserated with his colleagues. When he overheard them complaining, he encouraged them to see the bigger picture of the company. "I asked them to put themselves in the shoes of leadership. That's what I did, too," he said.

The result

Within a few months' time, Steven's boss called him into the office. He told Steven that the leadership team had noticed a change in Steven. They wanted to promote him to a leadership position. His new role was to help build a team of master craftsmen.

"They came to me with a new job description and a title to go along with it. I was now the head of quality."

Steven's vision had come true. He was to spend his days using his years of experience and expertise to teach others how to build the highest quality products and not settle for mediocre.

"It was unbelievable," he recalled. "The bosses that I previously thought were unfair, now were fantastic! And I'm now excited to go to work," he said.

Steven's new role of wasn't his only promotion. A few months later, he received another promotion – the second one in less than one year.

How could this be? Steven didn't change bosses. He didn't change companies. His projects didn't change. The team didn't change.

So, what changed, I asked Steven.

"My mindset changed," he said.

Steven's story began with a sense of feeling out of control. He discovered the one thing that he could control: his thinking.

"I didn't even realize I was like that," Steven said, referring to his former way of thinking. "I was trapped in an employee mindset.

"Once I had awareness of it, then I could change it. I learned about the consultant mindset."

Steven was in the business of taking a piece of wood and shaping into something spectacular. He now was doing the same work on the inside. He was learning to shape his thoughts in order to create the spectacular life he had envisioned.

Will he start his own business someday? Who knows? But for now, a simple change in thinking created the joy he was looking for all along.

STOP THINKING LIKE AN EMPLOYEE
Key Points:

Employee mindset focuses on what you get

Consultant mindset focuses on what you give

If you focus on giving, the receiving is imminent

How can I add value to an organization using my unique skills, talents and abilities?

_____

_____

_____

_____

_____

_____

_____

_____

_____

_____

_____

_____

_____

_____

Action Steps:

List 3 steps you can take to add value to your "biggest client."

STOP THINKING LIKE AN EMPLOYEE
Additional Notes:

Chapter 2

Give Your Attention

The employee mindset focuses on getting attention.

The consultant mindset focuses on giving attention.

The consultant mindset focuses on what you give. The first step is to give your attention. This means paying attention to ways you can add value and help your client win the game.

Conversely, the employee mindset focuses on getting attention. This is a scarcity mindset that's fixed on, "what about me?" In this scenario, the employee mindset sees co-workers as competitors and is always on the lookout for getting what's owed him or her.

If you want to show up with a consultant mindset focused on adding value to your biggest client, you can't skip this first step of paying attention.

Adding value doesn't happen by default. If you're not paying attention, distractions will rob you of opportunities to add value that are right in front of you.

When my adorable Godson first signed up for t-ball a few years ago, those games were a riot! That little guy stayed so busy out in right field.

His first priority was to pick up dirt from the infield, dump it onto the bill of his cap, tip his head forward and watch the dirt pour into his glove. Next on the agenda was to spin around like Wonder Woman until he became so dizzy, he stood like the Tower of Pisa and eventually tipped over.

STOP THINKING LIKE AN EMPLOYEE

He was so distracted that when the ball finally did come his way, he didn't even see it. It stopped right in front of his nose. He was so distracted from his purpose that he missed the play. He missed the opportunity that was right in front of him. He could have added great value and helped his client (i.e. his team) win the game.

It would have been beneficial for my Godson to give his attention to the pitcher, the batter or the location of the ball at all times.

So where should you place *your* attention? How can you find ways to add value to your biggest client?

Value is defined by the customer

As you give attention to ways you can add value, keep in mind that value is always defined by the customer.

This is one of the first principles I learned during my time spent in the Continuous Improvement industry. Continuous Improvement is a concept developed by Toyota Motor Corporation, also known as Toyota Production System (TPS).

Toyota teaches employees to constantly give their attention to ways they can add more value to customers. This means, they spend considerable time in focus groups, interviews, surveys and other means of finding out what customers want.

To add value to your "biggest client," you have to know what your biggest client finds most valuable.

Remember, value is defined by the customer. In this case, your customer is your leader, team members, or the organization at large.

How do you know what the client defines as valuable? The best way is to ask.

How can I help you?

One way to find out what the customer values, is simply to ask the question, "how can I help you today?"

This is a powerful question for a couple of reasons.

First, it gives the customer an opportunity to tell you what's valuable. Second, the question itself will be a delight to your biggest client.

The employee mindset asks "how can you help me?"

The consultant mindset asks "how can I help you?"

The employee walks into a leader's office to ask for a raise, time off, a better office, or help with handling an angry customer.

Imagine how many times a day leaders have to stop what *they're* doing to solve problems, make decisions and help others. It's draining. All day long people are asking for something.

Do you want to stand out and shine like the North Star? Walk into a leader's office and ask how they're doing. You will stop them in their tracks with delight. Very seldom, if ever, does someone walk into a leader's office to inquire about them.

Give your attention and uncover opportunities by asking your leader questions like:

What's the biggest challenge on your plate these days?

What's keeping you up at night?

How is your day going?

What new projects are coming down the pike?

Is there anything I can do for you?

I once followed this line of questioning with a leader who responded by opening up about some very real challenges she was experiencing both personally and professionally. I just listened.

When she finished talking, I asked one simple question: how can I help? To which she replied, "you just did."

From my perspective, all I did was offer a friendly ear. Value is always defined by the customer.

Adding value through root-cause problem-solving

Another way to add value and stand out from the crowd is to give attention to problems that others cannot see. These problems occur deep below the surface.

Oftentimes, the problem you see on the surface isn't the *real* problem.

Have you ever tried to solve a problem only to discover that it comes right back?

Anytime you hear your biggest client use a phrase like, "here we go again," you know there's a deeper root to the problem.

When I first bought my house, I took pride in my beautiful freshly mowed lawn. One week I mowed north to south. The next week I mowed east to west. Then diagonal. My yard was the envy of the neighborhood.

Each year in May, however, I'd wake up to a yellow polka-dotted lawn – EEK dandelions!

Being the new homeowner that I was, I'd get out the mower and take down those dreaded dandelions in one fell swoop. Then I'd sit back in delight.

But two days later, (enter Jaws movie soundtrack music) duuunnnnnnnn dun dun dun dun dun dun dun dun dun dun –they'd explode up through the ground out of nowhere.

I didn't get them at the root.

That's how many problems appear in business. Everyone is moving so quickly that teams often take the quickest action to solve a problem. But there's usually a deeper root-cause that doesn't get solved.

You can be the "value-add consultant" by going deep beneath the surface. You'll quickly earn a reputation as the person who makes life better for your "biggest client," i.e. your leader.

This is how you stand out from the crowd:

Ask "why"

A big key to identifying root-cause problems is asking questions.

Giving your attention means becoming as curious as a 3-year-old. If you've ever been around three-year-olds, you know they never stop asking, "why?"

"Why is the sky blue? Why is the grass is green? Why do I have a belly button? Why does it rain?"

Why? Why? Why?

Did you ever notice a child asks great questions about things we see every day?!

Developing the consultant mindset means you must build your curiosity muscles.

If something doesn't add up, ask "why." If you don't have clarity or understand a project, ask "why."

If things seem too complex, ask "why."

If efforts are being duplicated, ask "why?

Asking why will help you get to the root of a problem so you can solve it for good!

When you put on your opportunity goggles, you can spot value-add opportunities on a regular basis that others don't see. You'll quickly earn a reputation as the person who makes life easier for your "biggest client."

STOP THINKING LIKE AN EMPLOYEE

Key Points:

1. Value is defined by the customer.

2. Your customer is your boss, team, leaders and organization at large.

3. Put on your opportunity goggles. Watch for problems you can solve.

4. To help uncover opportunities, be as curious as a 3-year-old.

5. Ask "why."

6. The employee mindset asks "how can you help me?"

7. The consultant mindset asks "how can I help you?"

Action Steps:

1. Make a list throughout the day of areas that seem overly complex or unclear.
2. Ask Why.
3. Leader/team check-in: Make it a daily practice to ask a leader or team member:
   - How are you doing today?
   - Is there anything I can do for you?

STOP THINKING LIKE AN EMPLOYEE
Additional Notes:

MARIANNE RENNER

Chapter 3

Give Solutions

Now that you've given attention to what's going on around you and uncovered problems, your next step as the consultant is to give solutions.

The employee mindset *gets* solutions, asking others to solve their problems.

The consultant *gives* solutions, offering help to others.

You've gone through the first step. You identified the problem.

The next step is to use your unique talents, gifts and abilities to solve it.

Use your unique talents, gifts and abilities to solve the problem.

When I started my coaching business, I was still working as a traditional W2 employee. My organization was in the process of closing our department due to a restructuring.

I started my business in preparation of my transition out of the organization.

During the transition period I took on a variety of project management duties. This meant regular meetings with leaders of various departments.

Wearing my opportunity goggles, I started noticing repeated conversations around the topic of employee engagement.

Employee engagement is a common challenge in corporate America. I found myself having similar conversations with my coaching clients around their own level of engagement in their roles. We were solving their problems and increasing their engagement.

I knew the solution. I also knew I had the abilities and skills to provide it.

I started by offering a leadership development workshop. From there, I provided individual coaching sessions with several supervisors and managers to help them engage their teams and improve their survey scores. We were able to pinpoint specific reasons for low engagement scores. We went to work and improved those scores.

Those last days in the organization were some of the most rewarding days in my tenure at the organization. An employee mindset would have said, "just coast on out the door." A consultant mindset never stops adding value.

Elizabeth's Story

One of my clients learned the power of problem-solving and landed herself unexpectedly in the top role of her organization.

Elizabeth was a director of operations for a multi-million-dollar organization.

When the company's CEO stepped down, the Board of Directors looked to her for a recommendation for the next CEO. She saw an opportunity to add value.

She did more than recommend a new CEO. She solved a bigger problem.

She knew the organization's challenges. She knew the weak spots. She knew her unique gifts, talents and abilities.

She had a gift for spotting the talents of others. She paid attention and saw what made others thrive.

She knew that the current structure of the organization wasn't tapping into the gifts and unique abilities of each team member.

She proposed a restructuring that would put each person in the right role for the greatest impact based on their unique talents.

She delivered a proposal that re-structured job duties for each staff member based on each person's strengths, talents and unique gifts. The new structure included her as CEO.

But she went even further. Knowing that her primary duty was to add the greatest value to the organization, she provided the board with a second option. The second option did not include her in the CEO position.

She didn't let her ego get in the way. She didn't focus on what she would get. Her primary focus was on what she could give.

She knew value is defined by the customer. Even though *she* believed she would be the best CEO, she knew the customer would want two options to choose from. With the customer in mind, she gave them a second option.

Her customer ultimately saw her as the greatest value for the company. The Board named her Chief Executive Officer.

The customer made the right decision. Elizabeth stepped in to her new role and restructured the organization. They had one of their best years after that.

When giving solutions, be ready to provide multiple solutions if the first one doesn't work. Your job as a consultant is to make life as easy as possible for your clients. They'll want a plan A, and a plan B.

STOP THINKING LIKE AN EMPLOYEE

Key Points

1. The employee gets solutions, asking leaders for help.
2. The consultant gives solutions, contributing answers and ideas.
3. Use your unique talents, gifts and abilities to solve the problem
4. Provide multiple solutions in case the first one is rejected or doesn't work.
5. Your job as a consultant is to make life easier for your biggest client.

Action Steps:

List 3 opportunities or problems to be solved with your biggest client.

_____

_____

_____

_____

_____

_____

Using your list of unique skills, list 2 solutions for each problem.

_____

_____

_____

_____

_____

_____

_____

_____

STOP THINKING LIKE AN EMPLOYEE
Additional Notes:

MARIANNE RENNER

Chapter 4

Give the L-Factor

People do business with people they know, like, and trust. A smart business owner knows that.

If you want to stand out from the crowd, give the L-Factor.

Likeability is proven to be one of the greatest differentiators for success. The more likeable you are, the greater the odds you'll be chosen for the best projects, the promotion, or the new job.

The employee mindset gives little thought to likeability.

The consultant mindset gives likeability.

Just how do you give the L-Factor? Those with a consultant mindset give likeability by starting with intention. They start by creating a personal brand.

Create your Personal Brand

During my career in the marketing/communications industry, one of my favorite parts of the job involved brand strategy. Developing a brand is exciting and inspiring.

The greatest companies have strong brands, and so can you.

People are loyal to their favorite brands. They pay more money for their favorite brands. They talk about their brands and refer them to others.

Doesn't that sound like something you'd like for your career or business?

STOP THINKING LIKE AN EMPLOYEE

What is a brand?

A brand is much more than a product or service name.

Target isn't just a department store. It's the place you can count on to buy high quality products at great value.

Mountain Dew isn't just a lemon-lime soft drink. It's the beverage that creates excitement and turns you into an extreme sports athlete.

When you think of brands like Nike or Amazon, you get an image in your mind. That image *is* the brand.

A brand is the real estate that a product or service takes up in the mind of the consumer.

When companies create brand strategies, they think about multiple elements. Logo, ad color, copywriting, tone, product design, and store layout - all of these elements work together to create a brand image.

To build a personal brand around your likeability factor, think about the many elements required to create that brand.

Elements to consider when building your likeability factor

What tone do you use in your emails? How do you respond to requests that are outside the scope of your work? What type of body language do you demonstrate at a meeting? Do you smile? Do you listen well? How do you dress?

All of these elements work together to create your personal brand of likeability.

You have a brand whether you know it or not.

Remember, a brand exists in the mind of the customer.

Let's say an airline, for example, creates an ad campaign around its great customer service. If customers experience long flight delays, extra service fees, and a stressful boarding process, what's the actual brand?

The brand is what the customer says it is. It's based on customer experience and the image in the customer's mind.

What do you want people to say about you when you're not in the room?

You're creating a personal brand, whether you realize it or not. People are talking about you.

They're creating opinions. You're taking up real estate in the mind of your customers. What are they saying about you when you're not in the room?

What do you *want* them to say when you're not in the room?

You'll want to be intentional about creating your L-factor brand.

Kenneth's Story

Several years ago, a client I had been working with was facing a layoff and wanted to plan his next steps. His company, a multi-billion-dollar manufacturing company, was going through a restructuring and a reduction in workforce.

Unfortunately, his position was one of the many casualties.

It was especially challenging for Kenneth (not his real name) for several reasons.

First of all, Kenneth loved this job. He and I had previously worked together to help him land this role. He loved the work, he loved the organization, and he loved his team. He didn't want to leave.

Next, this was Kenneth's second layoff in less than three years due to restructuring at the same

STOP THINKING LIKE AN EMPLOYEE

organization. He originally landed a mid-level manager role in the organization about 18 months earlier. When that position was eliminated, he moved into this newly created role. And now *this* role, too, was on the chopping block.

You can imagine the emotional rollercoaster Kenneth was riding. Remember, he was a great employee. His team loved him.

He was a high-performer and really hard-worker in the organization. But that wasn't enough. Remember we said hard work and competency is always a given. Hard work and competency are not what make you stand out. They make you equal with others.

Wait, there's more. To pile salt in the wound, Kenneth's company asked him to play a key role in helping other employees who also were facing layoffs. Ouch!

"I was getting laid off. I had about a month-and-a-half left in my position," Kenneth recalled. "I was asked to represent the company during the layoffs and help others losing their jobs. My role was to provide comfort to those being laid off. Of course, I didn't like it."

In our coaching calls Kenneth and I talked about his personal brand. I already knew Kenneth had the L-Factor. It was part of the reason the organization hired him in the first place. It was also the reason the company saved him during the first layoff. During that first layoff 18 months prior, the company told Kenneth at the eleventh hour that they didn't want to lose him. They created a new role for him with a bigger title and higher pay.

Imagine, a company is downsizing. Yet leaders decide to create a position with more pay for an employee they were going to let go.

Kenneth's L-Factor delivered him from the first layoff. Could it work a second time?

I asked Kenneth, what did he want people to say about him when he's not in the room?

After a brief pause in conversation, he replied with one clear sentence: "I'm going to do the right thing even when it feels like the wrong thing is happening to me."

"Kenneth is the guy who does the right thing, no matter what."

What customer wouldn't love that brand?!

It wasn't easy. Kenneth told me during those coaching days, "people would stop me in the halls and say, 'I can't believe they're doing this to you. You don't deserve it after all you've done for this organization.'"

Kenneth confessed to me, "I wanted to say, 'yeah, I know!"

But he did not say, "yeah, I know." Instead, he replied, "I'm grateful for the opportunity this organization has given me. I've had a great experience here."

He would have been well within his right to agree with them. Was he tempted? Absolutely.

But he remembered his personal brand and stayed true to his L-Factor. He remained humble and grateful, doing the right thing even when the wrong thing was happening to him.

He applied for other roles that were available in the organization. He continued to help others through their layoffs. He stayed committed to showing up and serving with enthusiasm, even when it was difficult.

As the days ticked by and the clock wound down, the layoff date was imminent. Kenneth quietly hoped that doing the right thing would pay off and earn him

STOP THINKING LIKE AN EMPLOYEE

a rescue at the eleventh hour just as it did during the layoff 18 months earlier.

It didn't.

He packed up and went home. But before he had time to empty his boxes into his home office, he got the call. "Hey, Kenneth," the voice of one of the leaders said excitedly. "The senior leaders are talking about you. They're saying, 'get that guy back here!'"

High-level decision-makers who had never worked with Kenneth, we're hearing a buzz about how great he was. They were talking about his exceptional leadership and high degree of character. They already knew his excellent quality of work.

They brought him back. And like before, Kenneth earned *another* promotion and *another* significant salary increase – making it two salary increases in two years.

"There happened to be (a high-level leader) who said she wanted to be there when I was assisting the employees through their layoff," Kenneth recalled. "She was touched with how I worked with the staff. She's the one who introduced me to my new boss. She's really the one who made it happen," he said referring to the new role.

"It really wasn't anything I said. I wasn't trying to talk myself up," Kenneth said. "It was all because I committed to doing the right thing."

The thing about strong brands is they create buzz.

Kenneth created buzz with his L-Factor.

What do you want your brand to be? The more clearly you can articulate your brand, the easier it will be to create the brand. Here are a few words to help you get started:

1. Trust
2. Integrity

3. Accountability
4. Responsibility
5. Empathy

STOP THINKING LIKE AN EMPLOYEE

Key Points:

1. People do business with people they know, like and trust.
2. Likeability is one of the greatest differentiators for success.
3. A brand is what others think about a product or service. It's the real estate taken in the customer's mind.
4. People are loyal to their favorite brands. They pay more money for their favorite brands. They talk about their brands and refer them to others.
5. To create a brand around your L-factor, think of many elements including, body language, tone, facial expressions, helpfulness.

Action Steps:

Create one sentence to describe your brand.

_____

_____

_____

_____

_____

_____

What do you want people to say about you when you're not in the room?

_____

_____

_____

_____

_____

_____

_____

STOP THINKING LIKE AN EMPLOYEE
Additional Notes

Chapter 5

Give Gratitude

If you want to stand head and shoulders above the crowd, develop a general sense of gratitude about your work, your team, your leader and your organization. Remember, this is your biggest client!

An employee mindset gives complaints.

A consultant mindset gives thanks.

Imagine being in business. You're working with your biggest client. You go to lunch with some of the employees you've been hired to serve.

You start talking about how terrible the client is.

That's absurd. What do you think would happen?

What if you were the client, and you heard your consultant bad-mouthing you?

We all know someone who's been a member of the "I-can't-believe-they-did-that" club."

"They cut our benefits again. They took away our free donuts in the breakroom."

The employee mindset focuses on what's wrong.

The consultant mindset focuses on what's great.

A good business owner knows the importance of staying positive and staying grateful.

Remember Kenneth from the previous chapter? He certainly had every reason to talk about being wronged by the organization that laid him off.

But when colleagues tried to engage him in the "I can't believe it" club, he returned with words of gratitude for what the organization had done for him.

STOP THINKING LIKE AN EMPLOYEE

He gained great experience in his role. He earned a great salary to support his family. He had an opportunity to meet wonderful people.

By giving gratitude, Kenneth was adding value to the organization.

Remember, value is defined by the customer.

Do you think the customer, a CEO of a company, would find it valuable to have an employee be grateful and share that gratitude with others during a major restructuring and downsizing?

I'd imagine that would be every CEO's dream.

How it works

When my clients explain to me their current work situations and the pain they're experiencing, I ask them to identify 3 things they're grateful for in their work.

They assume they either heard me wrong or I heard them wrong.

"I just told you why I want to leave my job. Why would you ask me to identify 3 great things?"

I'm not trying to convince them to stay in their current role. In fact, more often than not, they eventually leave. But you've got to fix things where you're at to get to where you're going.

There are multiple benefits to doing this gratitude exercise daily.

1. **Practice adding value.** If you'd like to move to a new role or new organization, you'll want to develop your consultant mindset before you go. Otherwise, you'll eventually end up in the same place. Wherever you go, you'll take yourself with you. Learn to give gratitude now as a regular habit.

2. **Stop the bleeding.** If you're feeling unfulfilled, overwhelmed or angry, focusing on what's

wrong will only exacerbate the pain. If you shift your thinking to gratitude, you just start to feel better. You'll reduced the pain.
3. **What you focus on expands.** It may sound a little woo-woo, but many of my clients will tell you that as soon as they focused on things to be grateful for, more things to be grateful for started showing up in unexpected ways.

I had one client come to me because he was miserable in his job. He struggled with this exercise in gratitude toward his current organization. But after six months of giving gratitude for his current role, a dream role came seemingly out of nowhere. He said to me, "I have a new problem. I actually like where I am now." That's a great problem to have.

Another client I worked with spent 10 years in high-salaried position at a global tech firm where he had to drag himself out of bed every morning with no enthusiasm whatsoever.

He stayed because the pay was so great that he thought he'd never be able to do work that energized him at pay that sustained his family. As soon as he adopted the consultant mindset, an exciting up-and-coming company sought him out.

Giving gratitude is a rare and a highly sought-after quality by your potential "biggest clients."

Rachel's Story

Rachel is one of the most grateful human beings I have ever met. She was working in an insurance office when she came to me in search of finding more meaningful work.

STOP THINKING LIKE AN EMPLOYEE

"I've never known what I 'wanted to be when I grow up,'" Rachel recalled. "It was a terrible feeling to not know what I wanted to do."

Rachel told me a story about a special needs child who was asked the question, "what do you want to be when you grow up?"

"Grateful," he replied.

"Oh, how that resonated with me," Rachel said. "When you don't know what you want to be, you can always be grateful."

Rachel described her job at that time as being just "ok." She felt like she was meant for something more. She longed for a sense of meaning and fulfillment that was missing in her work.

In her search for meaning, she decided to start with gratitude.

"I was working as an office manager, and I was struggling with that feeling of not knowing what I bring to the table," she recalled. "With the help of coaching, I decided to let it go, she said, referring to worrying and a sense of unhappiness at work. "Instead, I started being grateful for what I had."

Things quickly changed.

Once she let go of her negative feelings about what she didn't have at work, and began to give gratitude, she surprisingly started to enjoy her work.

It was only a short time later that a new door of opportunity opened up. A former boss contacted her and offered her a position at a new company.

"I changed what I focused on. I started to ask myself, 'what good things can I focus on today?' Then out of nowhere, this new opportunity opened up," she said.

It was a paradox for sure. She stopped trying to get something. She gave gratitude for what she had.

Only then did she end up with a new and exciting opportunity.

STOP THINKING LIKE AN EMPLOYEE

Key Points:

1. An employee gives complaints. A consultant gives thanks.

2. Value is defined by the customer. Your customer values gratitude

3. Start developing a consultant mindset of gratitude right now in your current situation.

Action Steps:

Write 3 things you're grateful for each day in a dedicated gratitude notebook.

Try to look for new things each day. Did your computer break down? Don't focus on the breakdown. You can be grateful an IT specialist magically appeared to get you a new one. (Believe me, that doesn't happen for most consultants). something you're grateful for to your team or leader. You'll blow them away with unexpected delight.

STOP THINKING LIKE AN EMPLOYEE
Additional Notes:

MARIANNE RENNER

Chapter 6

Give Your Gifts

The consultant mindset asks: "where can I use my unique gifts, talents and abilities to and add value and solve problems for my client?"

A good business owner knows what makes him or her unique. In the world of marketing, this is called a UVP, or Unique Value Proposition. Businesses with a clear UVP are more valuable to customers.

You're more valuable when you have clarity on your unique gifts, skills, talents and abilities.

You bring a fresh perspective

One reason knowing your UVP makes you more valuable is you see opportunities from a fresh perspective. You see things that others may not see because you're looking through the lens of your unique gifts, talents and abilities.

Remember Elizabeth from the previous chapter on giving solutions? She saw an opportunity that only she could solve in her unique way. Elizabeth is what we would call a "people-person." She has a great ability to show empathy and cares deeply about the emotions of others

She has the unique ability to notice when people feel energized and engaged. She can tell when others are thriving, and she knows what makes them thrive.

When her board of directors asked for a fresh perspective on how to grow the organization, she saw an opportunity to help her team thrive. She knew that if her team members were energized, they would have a greater impact on the organization's bottom line. She proposed a new structure that would put people in roles that aligned with their greatest skills.

It worked. The board loved the idea. They named her CEO. Elizabeth created a culture where team members flourished.

You're more energized

When you're providing your unique talents, gifts, skills and abilities, you feel like the Energizer bunny. You're energized to the point where you could go on forever. You experience new levels of fulfillment. It becomes fun when you see an opportunity and solve a problem by using your UVP.

You begin to add value to your biggest client in a multitude of ways.

For one thing, you're solving the problem. What's more, you bring a fresh level of energy, which is contagious. Your energy and enthusiasm inspire others around you. And that's valuable!

Define your UVP

The previous chapters focus on adding value by using your unique gifts, talents and abilities. But what if you're not sure what those are?

Each person on planet earth is made for a unique purpose. You have gifts, talents and abilities that no one else can replicate.

It's not enough that I believe it. The more important question is, do YOU believe it? YOU have to believe you can add great value to the organization with unique gifts, talents and abilities.

Oftentimes my clients will say to me, "but how do I know what makes me unique? What if I don't have anything special to give?"

Yes, you most certainly do have something special to give! The answer is closer than you realize.

One reason people don't believe they have a unique purpose, is because one's purpose usually comes naturally. Because your purpose feels natural, you discount it. You overlook your valuable abilities.

A second reason people don't see their unique value is due to a lack of confidence or limiting belief. They've simply told themselves for too long that they don't have anything valuable to offer. By repeating that message over time, it becomes a belief.

Kyle's story

I once had a client who came to me because he was facing a job layoff. He was worried about not being able to provide for his family, and he didn't know where to go next with his career.

He told me that he had held a number of jobs, but none of them felt like the right fit. None of them added up to anything that looked like a career path, from his perspective.

When I asked him to tell me about his background, he said that he didn't have any real marketable skills.

He was discouraged. To help him gain confidence, I asked him to tell me about something in his career he was proud of.

The answer kept coming back, "nothing."

I knew from previous conversations that Kyle had earned his Bachelor's degree, landing a spot on the Dean's List. Moreover, he did this all while working

STOP THINKING LIKE AN EMPLOYEE

full-time AND running a profitable side business in the automotive industry.

"That's not something to be proud of?" I asked. He explained that his college business courses came very easy for him. He interpreted that to mean that his degree didn't really matter.

Many people discount skills that come easy for them. But it's this very point that makes your skills unique.

As it turns out, Kyle had not only one, but three possible career paths he could have chosen. He had achieved great success in continuous improvement, project management and marketing.

The unfortunate part of the story is that Kyle didn't recognize any of it. He discounted the skills that made him most unique.

If you are challenged to find your unique value, ask those closest to you to describe what they see about you. An outside set of eyes can be extremely helpful.

The action steps identified at the end of this chapter will offer you assistance in clarifying your UVP. After you work through the questions, you will begin to identify your unique skills, talents, gifts and abilities.

Your clarity may not come at once. The process may seem be more like that of a sculptor who gradually begins to see an image emerge as he sculpts away the unnecessary clay.

This final piece is so important in developing the consultant mindset. If you're simply trying to add value everywhere and anywhere, you'll burn yourself out.

You'll continue to feel like your job is draining your energy if you try to add value without recognize your unique gifts, talents and abilities.

When you know what makes your heart sing, you become energized in your work. Those around you become energized. You become fulfilled as you contribute in a fresh and meaningful way.

Kenneth's Story Continued

In chapter 4 you met Kenneth, who survived two job layoffs because of his likeability factor.

What you didn't learn was how he came to understand his unique gifts, skills and abilities.

When Kenneth first came to me, he was working in a small office as a program coordinator with no sense of fulfillment from his work.

"My job is sucking the life energy out of me," were his exact words when he first approached me about coaching.

I asked him, "what would you rather be doing in your career?"

"I don't know," was his reply.

He knew he wasn't happy where he was, but he didn't know where he wanted to go.

He recalled one of his first assignments in coaching.

"I highlighted my favorite parts of all my past job descriptions," he recalled. "Themes and ideas started popping out. I began focusing on what I loved to do, instead of what seemed like I 'should do.'"

Kenneth explained that his biggest breakthrough came from shifting his mindset to what he called an "inside-out approach."

"I used to approach a job search from the outside, in. I was always focusing externally – what other people said I should do, what job titles looked right, or what looked good from the outside," he recalled.

STOP THINKING LIKE AN EMPLOYEE

"Instead, I started asking, do I love this? What feels good on the inside?"

Kenneth noticed that even though he wasn't happy in his past work roles, there were bits and pieces of every job that he enjoyed. The common theme was teaching and working with others.

Not long after that first exercise of listing out characteristics of work he loved, a job opportunity showed up, seemingly out of nowhere.

"When I was first looking for another job, I was so focused on what my qualifications looked like on paper. I almost didn't apply for this particular role," he remembered.

He was stuck on the fact that his formal education didn't seem to match the job. "I didn't see the connection," he said.

But the job description was a perfect match for the kind of work that made Kenneth's heart sing.

He applied and landed the role, designing and delivering training programs for employees.

He doubled his salary and found it to be a dream job.

"I stopped focusing on the external (reasons that I shouldn't apply). I already had what it took for that job," he said.

One year later, his company custom-designed a new role for him with a bigger title and significant pay increase. (Remember the layoff story from the previous chapter?)

That role, too, was a perfect fit.

Kenneth ultimately found himself doing work as a professional facilitator. He's now facilitating discussions among groups to help teams meet their goals.

"Ten years ago, or even one year ago, I never would have said, 'I want to be a group facilitator.' But I kept focusing on the next step in front of me."

Today, C-suite leaders are requesting Kenneth to facilitate their meetings and showering him with accolades for the work he's doing.

More importantly, the work he does feels as natural as breathing, he says.

Kenneth explains that it wasn't easy to first identify what made him unique. "We don't notice our unique gift because it's natural. It's like breathing – you don't notice you're doing it."

For anyone feeling stuck and challenged with identifying their unique gift, Kenneth recommends starting with the inside-out approach.

Lean in to what you love, he suggests. Then focus on the next step in front of you.

"One thing that really helped me in coaching was shifting my focus from 'how can I do a good job,' to 'how can I serve,'" he said. "I stay focused on using my gift to serve."

Today, Kenneth no longer feels like his job is sucking his life energy from him. Rather, he feels empowered.

"Looking back, I was an employee. I didn't feel like I was in control of what I contributed. It was about whatever my boss told me to do. It was his vision, his action items. It had nothing to do with my gifts and talents.

"Now, I feel empowered to lean into my own gifts and serve the team uniquely."

Kenneth is now working on his next role. He's working on it from the inside out, visioning how he can lean into his talents as a gifted facilitator to serve even more people in a greater capacity.

STOP THINKING LIKE AN EMPLOYEE

Kenneth's journey has been one of transformation. His greatest learning has been to shift his mindset.

"The only limits that are real and holding you back are the limits you create in your mind," he says. You have the power to create your limits, and you have the power to take them down."

Key Points:

1. You have a unique purpose with unique talents, gifts and abilities.

2. To add the greatest value to your biggest client, use your unique gifts, talents and abilities.

3. It can be difficult to see your own unique gifts because they come natural to you.

4. Great businesses define what makes them unique by clarifying their UVP (unique value proposition).

5. Use the action steps below to help you define your UVP.

STOP THINKING LIKE AN EMPLOYEE
Action Steps:

Ask others
> Ask three people who know you to tell you what they value most about you. Keep asking why to flush out the uniqueness. What makes you stand out in their eyes? What do they think makes you unique? What's the first thing they think of when they think of you?

What comes natural?
> What feels so joyful to you that you could do it all day long? It's as natural as breathing. What leaves you feeling fulfilled?

What do people ask you for?
> More than likely, people come to you for help because of your unique gifts.

Journal.
> Dedicate a notebook specifically for this action step. List every job you've ever had. Next to each job, write out all the characteristics that made your heart sing. What got you excited? What puts a smile on your face when you think of it.

> It's important for this step that you don't self-edit. It's ok of the characteristics don't match from job to job. It's ok if they don't "seem" like something viable or profitable. Writing a free-flow of thoughts is key. You're looking for themes to emerge.

Say it out loud.
> Have a conversation with someone and talk about what gets you jazzed up about your previous or current work. Ask the other person

to take notes and write down key phrases that stand out.

STOP THINKING LIKE AN EMPLOYEE
Additional notes:

MARIANNE RENNER

Chapter 7

Putting it all together

Rachel's full story

Remember Rachel, the most grateful person on the planet? Giving gratitude was just one step in her journey toward finding meaningful work.

Rachel remembers, "I just didn't know what kind of work I wanted to do. I didn't know what made me unique or what special gifts I have to offer." She described that period in her life. "I just wasn't being myself, and that it was a terrible feeling.

"I remember learning during my coaching sessions that the answer is inside me, and we just have to bring it out."

And that's what happened.

Through a journey of self-exploration, Rachel learned that she was a natural encourager. When she looked back at previous jobs and other aspects of her life, she noticed that she always felt lighter and more fulfilled when she was encouraging others.

"I discovered that no matter what job I have or profession I work in, I can share my personal gift to encourage and empower people around me."

Rachel explains that some days, encouragement means offering a warm smile. On other days it's giving a word of inspiration to her team.

STOP THINKING LIKE AN EMPLOYEE

She started her journey by giving gratitude, then discovered her gift of encouragement. She started acting on both of those while she remained in her job as an office manager.

L-Factor

Rachel discovered another gift that she didn't realize she had. She has a huge L-Factor. Rachel is extremely likeable. Anytime you give gratitude and encourage people around you, you can't help but raise your L-Factor.

With Rachel's triple-threat: giving gratitude, giving the L-Factor, AND giving her unique gifts, the inevitable happened.

Opportunity knocked on the door. Rachel answered.

One of Rachel's former leaders called and offered her a leadership position at a new company with twice the pay. About a year after that, she was promoted to Vice President in her company.

"I no longer had to search for the job or for meaning. The new job came searching for me" she said.

Rachel believes that her shift in attitude played an enormous role in her new opportunity. "I started to change what I focused on. Once I started focusing on the value I could bring and the good I could do for someone else, then this opportunity opened up," she said.

She had made such an impression on her former boss, he told her, "I knew I wanted to work with you again one day."

In fact, Rachel is beginning to notice this recurring theme of people wanting to work with her. "I just got a call from someone who used to work with me. She's interested in a position at our company, but she said, 'I only want to come there if I can work for you.'"

Another former team member under Rachel's leadership left the organization to pursue an opportunity that was too good to pass by. "I was supportive of her decision. I wanted her to be happy," Rachel recalled, adding, "then one year later she came back. She said it's just too good working for you."

Rachel is intentional about raising her L-Factor. She follows what she calls, "the Golden Rule."

"Everyone wants to feel important," she says. "I learn about people and what makes them feel important. I take an interest in them and make them feel important. I treat them the way I would want to be treated."

Rachel also believes in building trust and rapport with her team and leaders. "I focus on being honest and transparent," she says. "People want you to be direct. They appreciate your transparency."

This is all part of adopting the consultant mindset, Rachel says.

She laughs now as she looks back. "When I met you (her coach), I griped a lot! But I decided it wasn't doing me any good. I knew I needed to do something different, so I made a choice to change."

Adopting a consultant mindset doesn't always end up in landing a dream job right away. But it does pay dividends.

Rachel acknowledges that she hasn't quite found that ideal career.

"I don't feel like I'm in my final profession," she says. "I'm still in the same industry. But I feel so much differently about it."

The fact that Rachel is in the same industry, yet feels so much fulfillment, is an indication that she made a tremendous shift in her mindset.

STOP THINKING LIKE AN EMPLOYEE

"That's how I know something big happened from changing my mindset," she said. "Everything is different now in the way I feel."

Rachel attributes her change to adopting the consultant mindset and shifting her focus from what she wants to get, to what she can give.

"People don't understand how much value they can bring to their work. They're so valuable. Rather than try to get something, focus on what you can give," she said. "You get so much more when you give."

"I made a choice to change – not with work, but within. I made a choice to grow myself. And when I changed, everything changed."

Conclusion

Millions of people across the United States show up to work every day with an employee mindset. As a result, they're left feeling unfulfilled, overwhelmed, stressed out and generally unhappy for at least half of their waking hours.

To pile on the pain, they're underpaid and undervalued. But that's because they haven't tapped in to their consultant mindset.

When you make an internal shift and show up with a more empowered mindset, everything around you changes.

You may think you would be happy if only you could change your boss, change your company, or change other circumstances around you.

But the truth is, when you change first, everything around you changes.

The client stories in the preceding chapters are true stories. They're not isolated cases.

One thing they all have in common, is they had help. Developing a new mindset is not an easy thing to do alone. We all have blind spots. An outside set of eyes can help us see things we cannot.

I'd like to invite you to check out my Chaos to Clarity Mastermind group. / MarianneRenner.com / Mastermind. This is a group of likeminded individuals who come together for support and growth. Mastermind members experience exponential growth from the synergy created by the group.

STOP THINKING LIKE AN EMPLOYEE

Here are a few additional tips to help you start developing a consultant mindset today.

Before every workday and before each meeting, take 10 minutes and do the following:

1. Breathe deeply
2. See yourself as a consultant
3. Remind yourself of your unique talents, skills, gifts, and abilities
4. Mentally put on your opportunity googles
5. Prepare yourself to give your attention, and ask questions to uncover opportunities, and offer solutions
6. Read over your personal brand statement, and commit to building your likeability-factor
7. Give gratitude for 3 things each day

You may not see a change tomorrow, but you will see a change.

Your change might show up in the form of a promotion that comes seemingly out of nowhere. It might show up in the form of a new job at another organization. Perhaps you'll become so adept at thinking like a business owner, that you'll start a thriving new business.

As you change your mindset, people will start noticing the change. You'll be in high demand.

You'll wake up one day and suddenly realize you feel a greater sense of fulfillment.

When you start to see change on the outside, you'll know that the greatest work you've done is on the inside. External circumstances are like signs along a cross-country road trip. They're telling you you're on the right path or you've taken a detour.

Right now, you may be on a detour. Start to develop the consultant mindset, and you'll soon find yourself soaring down the highway.

Additional Resources

Below is a list of additional tools to help you build your consultant mindset and overcome limiting beliefs that may be keeping you stuck.

Download and access any of the following resources:

4 Ways You May Be Sabotaging Your Success
MarianneRenner.com/sabotage

Join the Chaos to Clarity private online community for leaders
Facebook.com/groups/MoveFromChaosToClarity

Limiting Beliefs Worksheet
MarianneRenner.com/belief

Goals with Purpose worksheet
MarianneRenner.com/Goals

Chaos to Clarity Mastermind
MarianneRenner.com/mastermind

About the Author

Marianne Renner is a highly sought-after leadership coach, trainer and speaker who helps aspiring and emerging leaders eliminate limiting beliefs so they can lead with more confidence and courage. Her live coaching and training programs include the Chaos to Clarity Leadership Academy, Facilitation Certification Program, DISC Behavior Training: Change the Direction of Your Connection, and additional mastermind and group programs. You can learn more about Marianne and her programs at www.MarianneRenner.com.

Or follow her at:

facebook.com/groups/MoveFromChaostoClarity

facebook.com/MarianneRennerCoachingSolutions

Additional notes:

STOP THINKING LIKE AN EMPLOYEE

MARIANNE RENNER

STOP THINKING LIKE AN EMPLOYEE

STOP THINKING LIKE AN EMPLOYEE

MARIANNE RENNER

STOP THINKING LIKE AN EMPLOYEE

MARIANNE RENNER

STOP THINKING LIKE AN EMPLOYEE

MARIANNE RENNER

Made in United States
North Haven, CT
21 January 2022